PRESIDENT TRUMP'S 1ST 100 DAYS
IN OFFICE..."TOUGH LOVE"

PRESIDENT TRUMP'S 1ST 100 DAYS IN OFFICE..."TOUGH LOVE"

PAUL YOUNG

ISBN-13: 9781548227791
ISBN-10: 154822779X
Library of Congress Control Number: 2017913412
CreateSpace Independent Publishing Platform
North Charleston, South Carolina

CONTENTS

PREFACE

Over sixty-two million Americans voted for Donald J. Trump to become the forty-fifth president of the United States of America. Whether you love him or hate him, he is our president. Ask yourself this: What is the worst thing that could happen to the United States of America with Donald J. Trump as president? Take an honest look at where this country was on January 20, 2017, when he took office, and the hundredth day, on April 29, 2017, and compare what Trump stated as campaign promises to what he has accomplished in the first one hundred days. Trump has always stated his intentions and goals for the United States of America:

"We will make America strong again."
"We will make America wealthy again."
"We will make America proud again."
"We will make America safe again."
"We will make America great again."

Chapter 1

TRUMP WILL NOT WIN ELECTION

When Donald J. Trump announced his intent to run for the White House, he was considered an underdog. His chance of winning the presidency was improbable. When he won the Republican nomination, some Americans became nervous and concerned that he had a chance to win against Hillary Clinton. The press was no help to his campaign with the headlines they produced.

June 21, 2016
The Nation
"Relax, Donald Trump Can't Win"
"Even before you get to his campaign's incompetence and lackluster fundraising, the numbers just aren't on his side."

June 11, 2016
The Guardian
"Trump Won't Win. In Fact, the US Could Be on the Brink of a Liberal Renaissance"
"With voters set to reject their nominee, Republicans could lose control of Congress, ushering in a progressive era."

August 12, 2016
Politico
"GOP Insiders: Trump Can't Win"
"'Trump is underperforming so comprehensively...it would take video evidence of a smiling Hillary drowning a litter of puppies while terrorists surrounded her with chants of "Death to America,"' said an Iowa Republican."

February 17, 2016
BBC News
"'Donald Trump will not be president,' says Barack Obama."
"Republican Donald Trump will not be president because it's a 'serious job.'"

October 28, 2016
Silver Doctors
"If Donald Trump wins the election, it will be the biggest miracle in US political history."
"And without a doubt Donald Trump desperately needs something 'to move the needle,' because if the election was held today Hillary Clinton would almost certainly win."

September 29, 2016
The Editorial Board, *USA Today*
USA Today's editorial board: "Trump is 'unfit for the presidency.'"
"We haven't made a voting recommendation in 34 years. For the election, we made an exception. We're doing it now."

Chapter 2

CAMPAIGN PROMISES

Donald Trump made the following promises during his campaign:

* Increase border security, and give law enforcement and border patrol the tools they need to fight illegal immigration.
* Make our military strong again.
* Build a wall, and Mexico will pay for it.
* Terminate President Obama's executive orders related to immigration.
* Temporarily ban Muslims from entering the United States.
* Bring manufacturing jobs back.
* Keep plants from leaving the United States.
* Impose tariffs on goods made in China and Mexico.
* Renegotiate our trade deals.
* Renegotiate or withdraw from the North American Free Trade Agreement (NAFTA) and Trans-Pacific Partnership (TPP).
* Repeal and replace Obamacare.
* Renegotiate the Iran deal.
* Lower the corporate-tax rate.
* Cut taxes for all.
* Leave Social Security alone.
* Destroy ISIS, radical Islamic terrorism.

* Issue a moratorium on new federal regulations.
* Rescind all environmental executive actions signed by Obama.
* Eliminate intrusive regulations.
* Be the greatest jobs president that God ever created.
* Don't take the presidential salary of $400,000.
* Bar Syrian refugees from entering the country.
* Set up safe zones in Syria.
* Take care of our infrastructure.
* Drain the swamp in Washington.
* Instruct the attorney general to appoint a special prosecutor to investigate Hillary Clinton.
* Get rid of Common Core.
* Provide school choice.
* Rebuild and fix inner cities.
* Support law and order.
* Back the police.
* Pick Supreme Court justices who are really great legal scholars.
* End political correctness.
* Say "Merry Christmas" again.
* Defund Planned Parenthood because of abortion.
* Allow concealed-carry permits to be recognized in all fifty states.
* Start winning again, and winning like you've never seen before.
* Ask Congress to pass "Kate's Law," named for Kate Steinle (illegal immigrant crackdown).
* Immediately deport undocumented immigrants who have committed a crime, are a member of a gang, or pose a security threat.
* Create "extreme vetting" of all immigrants.
* Be unpredictable, and keep all military strategy secret.
* Get great generals like General Patton and General Douglas MacArthur.

* Examine cybersecurity.
* Put America first. Hire American; buy American.
* Get rid of gun-free zones at military bases, recruiting centers, and in some cases schools.
* Fix the rigged system; don't trust the media's fake news.

Chapter 3

ELECTION RESULTS

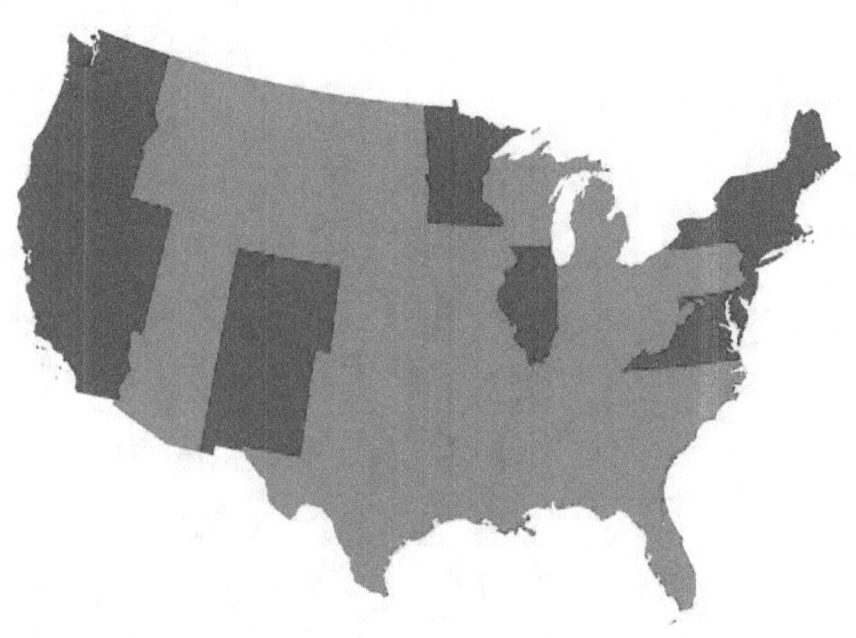

DONALD TRUMP—REPUBLICAN

Popular Vote	62,984,825
Percentage	46.09 percent
Electoral Votes	306

HILLARY CLINTON—DEMOCRATIC

Popular Vote	65,853,516
Percentage	48.18 percent
Electoral Votes	232

The table below contains the electoral votes that were won by each presidential candidate from each state.

STATE	TRUMP	CLINTON
Alabama	9	—
Alaska	3	—
Arizona	11	—
Arkansas	6	—
California	—	55
Colorado	—	9
Connecticut	—	7
Delaware	—	3
District of Columbia	—	3
Florida	29	—
Georgia	16	—
Hawaii	—	4
Idaho	4	—
Illinois	—	20
Indiana	11	—
Iowa	6	—
Kansas	6	—
Kentucky	8	—
Louisiana	8	—

Maine	1	3
Maryland	—	10
Massachusetts	—	11
Michigan	16	—
Minnesota	—	10
Mississippi	6	—
Missouri	10	—
Montana	3	—
Nebraska	5	—
Nevada	—	6
New Hampshire	—	4
New Jersey	—	14
New Mexico	—	5
New York	—	29
North Carolina	15	—
North Dakota	3	—
Ohio	18	—
Oklahoma	7	—
Oregon	—	7
Pennsylvania	20	—
Rhode Island	—	4
South Carolina	9	—
South Dakota	3	—
Tennessee	11	—
Texas	38	—
Utah	6	—
Vermont	—	3
Virginia	—	13
Washington	—	12
West Virginia	5	—
Wisconsin	10	—
Wyoming	3	—

Chapter 4

THE UNITED STATES' FINANCIAL/ POPULATION STATUS ON JANUARY 20, 2017

Donald J. Trump took office on January 20, 2017, and the key financial data of the United States of America is listed below for day one of his presidency. After one hundred days of the Trump presidency, you will be able to compare the key financial data of the United States of America and see if his presidency was positive or negative on the country (located on chapter 8).

US Population	325,419,703
US Workforce	152,224,972
Official Unemployed	7,507,202
Actual Unemployed	14,634,799
US Trade Deficit	$737,125,592,000
US National Debt	$19,962,116,270,000
Debt per Citizen	$61,346
Debt per Taxpayer	$166,773
Mortgage Rate	4.18 percent (Thirty-year fixed)
Unemployment Rate	4.7 percent
Inflation Rate	2.1 percent
US Savings Rate	5.50 percent
Dow	19827.25
S+P 500	2271.31
NASDAQ	5555.33

Chapter 5

INAUGURAL SWEARING-IN AND
FULL INAUGURAL SPEECH

Donald Trump on Friday, January 20, 2017, came to the Capitol, where he placed his left hand on an old Bible used by Abraham Lincoln, raised his right hand, and repeated thirty-five words (plus his full name) read by Chief Justice John G. Robert Jr. from the Constitution: "I, Donald John Trump, do solemnly swear that I will faithfully execute the office of president of the United States and will to the best of my ability, preserve, protect, and defend the Constitution of the United States."

Then he made his inaugural speech from the presidential podium:

Chief Justice Roberts, President Carter, President Clinton, President Bush, President Obama, fellow Americans, and people of the world: Thank you.

We, the citizens of America, are now joined in a great national effort to rebuild our country and to restore its promise for all of our people.

Together, we will determine the course of America and the world for years to come.

We will face challenges. We will confront hardships. But we will get the job done.

Every four years, we gather on these steps to carry out the orderly and peaceful transfer of power, and we are grateful to President Obama and First Lady Michelle Obama for their gracious aid throughout this transition. They have been magnificent.

Today's ceremony, however, has very special meaning. Because today we are not merely transferring power from one administration to another, or from one party to another—but we are transferring power from Washington, DC, and giving it back to you, the American People.

For too long, a small group in our nation's capital has reaped the rewards of government while the people have borne the cost. Washington flourished—but the people did not share in its wealth. Politicians prospered—but the jobs left, and the factories closed.

The establishment protected itself, but not the citizens of our country. Their victories have not been your victories; their triumphs have not been your triumphs; and while they celebrated in our nation's capital, there was little to celebrate for struggling families all across our land.

That all changes—starting right here, and right now, because this moment is your moment: it belongs to you.

It belongs to everyone gathered here today and everyone watching all across America. This is your day. This is your celebration. And this, the United States of America, is your country.

What truly matters is not which party controls our government, but whether our government is controlled by the people. January 20th, 2017, will be remembered as the day the people became the rulers of this nation again. The forgotten men and women of our country will be forgotten no longer.

Everyone is listening to you now.

You came by the tens of millions to become part of a historic movement the likes of which the world has never seen before. At the center of this movement is a crucial conviction: that a nation exists to serve its citizens.

Americans want great schools for their children, safe neighborhoods for their families, and good jobs for themselves. These are the just and reasonable demands of a righteous public.

But for too many of our citizens, a different reality exists: mothers and children trapped in poverty in our inner cities; rusted-out factories scattered like tombstones across the landscape of our nation; an education system flush with cash, but which leaves our young and beautiful students deprived of knowledge; and the crime and gangs and drugs that have stolen too many lives and robbed our country of so much unrealized potential.

This American carnage stops right here and stops right now.

We are one nation—and their pain is our pain. Their dreams are our dreams; and their success will be our success. We share one heart, one home, and one glorious destiny.

The oath of office I take today is an oath of allegiance to all Americans.

For many decades, we've enriched foreign industry at the expense of American industry; subsidized the armies of other countries while allowing for the very sad depletion of our military; we've defended other nation's borders while refusing to defend our own; and spent trillions of dollars overseas while America's infrastructure has fallen into despair and decay.

We've made other countries rich while the wealth, strength, and confidence of our country has disappeared over the horizon.

One by one, the factories shuttered and left our shores, with not even a thought about the millions upon millions of American workers left behind.

The wealth of our middle class has been ripped from their homes and then redistributed across the entire world.

But that is the past. And now we are looking only to the future. We assembled here today are issuing a new decree to be heard in every city, in every foreign capital, and in every hall of power.

From this day forward, a new vision will govern our land.

From this moment on, it's going to be America first.

Every decision on trade, on taxes, on immigration, on foreign affairs will be made to benefit American workers and American families. We must protect our borders from the ravages of other countries making our products, stealing our companies, and destroying our jobs. Protection will lead to great prosperity and strength.

I will fight for you with every breath in my body—and I will never, ever let you down.

America will start winning again, winning like never before.

We will bring back our jobs. We will bring back our borders. We will bring back our wealth. And we will bring back our dreams.

We will build new roads, and highways, and bridges, and airports, and tunnels, and railways all across our wonderful nation.

We will get our people off of welfare and back to work—rebuilding our country with American hands and American labor.

We will follow two simple rules: Buy American, and hire American.

We will seek friendship and goodwill with the nations of the world—but we do so with the understanding that it is the right of all nations to put their own interests first.

We do not seek to impose our way of life on anyone, but rather to let it shine as an example for everyone to follow.

We will reinforce old alliances and form new ones—and unite the civilized world against radical Islamic terrorism, which we will eradicate completely from the face of the Earth.

At the bedrock of our politics will be a total allegiance to the United States of America, and through our loyalty to our country, we will rediscover our loyalty to each other.

When you open your heart to patriotism, there is no room for prejudice. The Bible tells us, "How good and pleasant it is when God's people live together in unity."

We must speak our minds openly, debate our disagreements honestly, but always pursue solidarity.

When America is united, America is totally unstoppable.

There should be no fear—we are protected, and we will always be protected.

We will be protected by the great men and women of our military and law enforcement, and, most importantly, we are protected by God.

Finally, we must think big and dream even bigger.

In America, we understand that a nation is only living as long as it is striving.

We will no longer accept politicians who are all talk and no action—constantly complaining but never doing anything about it.

The time for empty talk is over. Now arrives the hour of action.

Do not let anyone tell you it cannot be done. No challenge can match the heart and fight and spirit of America.

We will not fail. Our country will thrive and prosper again.

We stand at the birth of a new millennium, ready to unlock the mysteries of space, to free the Earth from the miseries of disease, and to harness the energies, industries, and technologies of tomorrow.

A new national pride will stir our souls, lift our sights, and heal our divisions.

It is time to remember that old wisdom our soldiers will never forget: that whether we are black or brown or white, we all bleed the same red blood of patriots, we all enjoy the same glorious freedoms, and we all salute the same great American Flag.

And whether a child is born in the urban sprawl of Detroit or the windswept plains of Nebraska, they look up at the same night sky, they fill their heart with the same dreams, and they are infused with the breath of life by the same almighty creator.

So to all Americans, in every city near and far, small and large, from mountain, and from ocean to ocean, hear these words:

You will never be ignored again.

Your voice, your hopes, and your dreams will define our American destiny. And your courage and goodness and love will guide us along the way.

Together, we will make America strong again.

We will make America wealthy again.

We will make America proud again.

We will make America safe again.

And yes, together, we will make America great again. Thank you. God bless you. And God bless America.

Chapter 6

THE CABINET

DONALD TRUMP'S SELECTED TEAM

Vice President
Mike R. Pence

Secretary of State
Rex W. Tillerson

Secretary of the Treasury
Steven T. Mnuchin

Secretary of Defense
General James Mattis

Attorney General
Senator Jeff Sessions

Secretary of the Interior
Ryan Zinke

Secretary of Agriculture
Sonny Perdue

Secretary of Commerce
Wilbur L. Ross Jr.

Secretary of Labor
Alex Acosta

Secretary of Health and Human Services
Tom Price

Secretary of Housing and Urban Development
Benjamin S. Carson Sr.

Secretary of Transportation
Elaine L. Chao

Secretary of Energy
James Richard Perry

Secretary of Education
Betsy DeVos

Secretary of Veterans Affairs
David J. Shulkin

Secretary of Homeland Security
General John F. Kelly

Cabinet-Level Officials

White House Chief of Staff	Reince Priebus
Ambassador of the United Nations	Nikki R. Haley
Administrator of the Environmental Protection Agency	Scott Pruitt
US Trade Representative	Robert Lighthizer
Director of the Office of Management and Budget	Mick Mulvaney
Chairman of the Council of Economic Advisers	Vacant
Administrator of the Small Business Administration	Linda E. McMahon
Director of National Intelligence	Daniel Coats
Director of Central Intelligence Agency	Mike Pompeo

Chapter 7

JANUARY 20, 2017, TO APRIL 29, 2017
(DAY 1 TO DAY 100)

JANUARY 20, 2017
DAY 1

* Donald J. Trump is sworn in as the forty-fifth president of the United States at noon at the Capitol.
* Trump issues executive order scaling back parts of Obamacare.

JANUARY 21, 2017
DAY 2

* President Donald Trump attends a national prayer service at Washington's National Cathedral.

  Over two dozen religious leaders from different faiths were in attendance. The interfaith ceremony will be in keeping with the uniting and uplifting inaugural events.

* President Donald Trump visits the CIA headquarters.

  "There is nobody that feels stronger about the intelligence community and the CIA than Donald Trump."

  "Your whole group, these are really special amazing people. Very, very few people could do the job you people do."

  "You are going get so much backing."

  "We have not used the real abilities that we have; we've been restrained."

  "We have to get rid of ISIS; we have to get rid of ISIS; we have no choice Radical Islamic Terrorism. This is evil; this is evil."

  "I met Mike Pompeo and that was the only guy I met. I didn't want to meet anybody else. You will be getting a total star; you are going be getting a total gem—you'll see."

  "We have to start winning again."

  "I am with you 100 percent."

  "I love honesty."

  "I like honest reporting."

  "I love you."

  "I respect you."

  "There's nobody I respect more; you are going to do a fantastic job and were going start winning again and you are going be leading the charge."

JANUARY 22, 2017
DAY 3

* President Donald J. Trump attends the White House senior staff swearing-in in the East Room (thirty assistants to the president).
* He addresses the newly sworn in team:

  "We're also a team; it's a team, a great team, a team that gets along. And as I said during my inaugural address, this is not about party; this is not about ideology. This is about country, our country, and it's about serving the American people. We're not here to help ourselves; we're here to devote ourselves to the national good. Public service is a high and great calling; it's our solemn duty together to protect the country, our country, this great great country. To defend its workers and promote the well-being of all Americans, so many people are depending on us and on you as families, you as people that are going get it done, so many people."

  "We will face many challenges, but with the faith in each other and the faith in God, we will get the job done. We will prove worthy of this moment in history, and I think it may very well be a great moment in history. So be proud; be very proud."
* Trump honors first responders.
* He announces upcoming meetings with the prime minister of the United Kingdom, Theresa May; the prime minister of Canada; and the president of Mexico, "who I know and we're going to start some negotiations having to do with NAFTA. But we're going start renegotiating on NAFTA, on immigration, and on security at the border, and Mexico has been terrific."

JANUARY 23, 2017
DAY 4

*   President Trump signs three presidential directives:
    Withdrawing US support for a Pacific Trade Deal (TPP) Trans-Pacific Partnership;
    Imposing a hiring freeze in civilian agencies, not including the military; and
    Restoring and expanding the so-called Mexico City Policy that prohibits US aid from supporting international groups that promote abortion.
*   President Trump meets with US business and union leaders about bringing jobs back to America and cutting regulations.

JANUARY 24, 2017
DAY 5

* President Trump signs a series of executive memorandums resurrecting the Keystone XL Pipeline and reviving the Dakota Access Pipeline and a directive ordering an end to protracted environmental reviews.
* Requiring American-made steel and changing the process of approving and regulating future pipeline and infrastructure projects.
* Meets with auto-industry representatives to discuss auto industry.

JANUARY 25, 2017
DAY 6

* President Trump signs two executive orders during a visit to the Department of Homeland Security.

  The first executive order calls for the construction of a large physical barrier on the southern border, "the wall."

  The second executive order reinstates the Secure Communities Program, which immigrants and Customs Enforcement (ICE) uses to target illegal immigrants for removal. It directs the State Department to withhold visas or take measures to ensure countries take back deported undocumented immigrants and also strips federal grant money from sanctuary cities that harbor undocumented immigrants.
* Cracks down on sanctuary cities.
* Empowers ICE officers to target and remove those who pose a threat to public safety.
* Calls for the hiring of another five thousand border patrol officers.
* Calls for tripling the number of ICE officers.
* Creates an Office of Homeland Security dedicated to supporting the victims of illegal immigrant crime.

  "Victims of immigrant crime open borders; we hear you; we see you, and you will never be ignored again."

  "When it comes to public safety, there is no place for politics, no Republicans, no Democrats, just citizens and good citizens. We want safe communities, and we demand safe communities for everyone. We want respect; we want great schools; we want dignity and equality for everyone. And I will be a President; I promise you for everyone."

JANUARY 26, 2017
DAY 7

* President Trump gives speech at GOP retreat in Philadelphia, Pennsylvania, and lays out his agenda:
  * Transfer power from Washington, DC, and give it back to the people.
  * Restore the rule of law.
  * Pursue new trade deals.
  * Bring back "made in the USA."
  * Create tax reform.
  * Create financial reform.
  * Rebuild this country with American goods and American labor.
  * Get people off welfare and back to work.
  * Develop infrastructure repair.
  * Rebuild our military, and take care of veterans.
  * Unleash the full power of American energy.
  * To become a rich country, we have to be a safe country.
  * Stand with the men and women of law enforcement.
  * Protect Americans from radical Islamic terrorism.
  * Protect the integrity of the ballot box.
  * Create a lean, efficient government.
  * Work every single day.
  * Make America great again.
* Signs executive order to build Keystone and Dakota pipelines.
* Signs executive order to use American steel to manufacture and fabricate here.
* Signs executive order to reinstate the Mexico City Policy.
* Signs executive order to remove wasteful regulations.
* Signs executive order to withdraw from TPP.
* Signs executive order repealing and replacing Obamacare.
* President Trump announces cancellation of meeting with the Mexican president for next week.

* President Trump proposes 20 percent import tax on Mexico to pay for the wall.
* Signs executive order instituting an immigration plan cracking down on sanctuary cities.
  "Congress passed these laws to serve our citizens and it's about time those laws our properly enforced."

JANUARY 27, 2017
DAY 8

* President Trump has a friendly hour-long phone call with the Mexican president.
* President Trump has press conference with UK prime minister Theresa May. Discusses foreign policy, Syria, Russia, NATO, and trade. Question-and-answer session with President Trump and Prime Minister Theresa May.
* President Trump attends James Norman Mattis's swearing-in ceremony at the Pentagon.
  He says, "Mattis is the right man at the right time."
* President Trump signs executive order about immigration relating to terrorism and new vetting measures regarding seven primarily Muslim countries: Iran, Iraq, Syria, Somalia, Sudan, Libya, and Yemen.
* President Trump signs executive order for military readiness: national security rebuilding of the military, new planes, new ships, new resources, and new tools for the men and women in uniform.
* President Trump signs executive order instituting a five-year ban on lobbying for administration officials.
* President Trump signs executive order for reorganization of National Security Council (NSC).
* President Trump signs executive order for the Pentagon to give a plan to defeat ISIS to President Trump in thirty days.

JANUARY 28, 2017
DAY 9

* President Trump speaks with Russian president Vladimir Putin. Discusses working together in Syria to target the Islamic State. Discusses the process of restoring economic ties between the two countries. Sanctions did not come up in call (trade, security, and efforts to defeat ISIS).
* President Trump has calls with multiple countries to discuss mutual issues.

JANUARY 29, 2017
DAY 10

* President Trump's immigration ban sends shock waves.
* A federal judge in Brooklyn blocks Presidents Trump's order on refugees amid chaos and outcry worldwide.

JANUARY 30, 2017
DAY 11

* President Trump signs executive order calling for the elimination of at least two regulations for each new one created.
* President Trump vows to dismantle the Dodd-Frank Act.
* President Trump meets with people of small businesses.
  "There are twenty-eight million small businesses in the country, and 48 percent hire small business workers."
  "Simplify and reduce regulations."
  "Simplify and lower taxes."
  "The American dream is back."
* President Trump fires acting attorney general Sally Yates. Yates betrayed the Department of Justice (DOJ) by refusing to enforce a legal order. President Trump names Dana Boente as acting attorney general.

JANUARY 31, 2017
DAY 12

* President Trump holds meeting led by Mayor Giuliani on cybersecurity experts.

* President Trump holds a breakfast-and-listening session with major pharmaceutical company executives.

* President Trump signs executive order on lesbian, gay, bisexual, transgender, and questioning (LGBTQ)workplace protections. The executive order signed in 2014 under President Obama, which protects employees from anti-LGBTQ workplace discrimination while working for federal contractors, will remain intact.

* President Trump and Vice President Pence attend the swearing-in ceremony for the new secretary of transportation, Elaine Chao.

* President Trump announces Neil Gorsuch as Supreme Court nominee.

FEBRUARY 1, 2017
DAY 13

* President Trump hosts a breakfast listening session as African American History Month begins.
* President Trump takes a trip to a Delaware military base to receive the remains of a US Navy Seal killed during a counterterrorism raid.
* President Trump meets with representatives regarding the Supreme Court nominee Gorsuch.
* President Trump will participate in a standing legislature affairs strategy meeting with his team, who have been working closely with Congress to enact the President's agenda.
* President Trump swears in Rex Tillerson as secretary of state.

FEBRUARY 2, 2017
DAY 14

* President Trump attends and gives a speech at the National Prayer Breakfast.

  "I am praying for you" (five words that inspire President Trump).

  "That is why I will get rid of and totally destroy the Johnson Amendment and allow our representatives of faith to speak freely and without fear of retribution."

* President Trump hosts a meeting-and-listening session with Harley-Davidson executives, union representatives, machinists, and steel workers to discuss industry and jobs.

FEBRUARY 3, 2017
DAY 15

* President Trump signs executive order on core principles for regulating the US financial system (reviews Dodd-Frank).
* President Trump signs executive order on fiduciary rule. This executive order rolls back financial regulations and returns to the American people their control of their own retirement savings.
* President Trump attends a strategic policy forum with business leaders.
* President Trump warns Israel about settlements.
* President Trump takes steps to address Iran's recent actions. Thirteen individuals and twelve entities are sanctioned that provide support to Iran's ballistic missile program/terror-related activities. The White House places new sanctions on Iran.
* Job report released: 227,000 new jobs created.
* Lockheed Martin renegotiates new lot of F35s, resulting in $455 million savings for US taxpayers and an average cost reduction of 7.5 percent.
* President Trump heads to Mar-a-Lago on Air Force One.

FEBRUARY 4, 2017
DAY 16

* President Trump is in Mar-a-Lago.
* President Trump slams the judge who blocked the immigration executive order. Judge James Robart had blocked travel ban.
  "The opinion of this so-called Judge, which essentially takes law enforcement away from our country, is ridiculous and will be overturned."
* Department of Justice (DOJ) appeals judge's order blocking President Trump's immigration ban.

FEBRUARY 5, 2017
DAY 17

* President Trump sits down for an exclusive interview with Bill O'Reilly of Fox News before the Super Bowl.
* The Ninth US Circuit Court of Appeals denies motion regarding travel ban.

FEBRUARY 6, 2017
DAY 18

* President Trump visits the headquarters of the US Central Command in Tampa, Florida, MacDill Air Force Base.

"Perhaps the only thing more important to me definitely is the defense of our nation."

"We will do that; believe me."

"No enemy stands a chance against our Special Forces, not even a chance; that is the way we're going keep it."

"We need strong programs so that people that love us and want to love our country and will end up loving our country are allowed in, not people that want to destroy us and destroy our country."

"Peace through strength."

"America first."

"Make America great again."

"We respect our flag."

"We honor our heroes."

FEBRUARY 7, 2017
DAY 19

* President Trump meets with US county sheriffs in the White House. "We're committed to securing our borders to reduce crime, illegal drugs, human trafficking. We're also committed to working with law enforcement to stop terrorist attacks. We're going be very tough on crime, we're going to be very tough on the drugs pouring in, we're going to be very strong at the border, we have no choice, and we're going to be building a wall; we're starting very soon. There's a new sheriff in town."

FEBRUARY 8, 2017
DAY 20

* President Trump waits on the decision of the Ninth US Circuit Court of Appeals to uphold his travel ban.
* President Trump makes a speech at the Major Cities Chiefs Association (MCCA) Winter Conference to address police chiefs from major cities.
* Intel CEO Brian Krzanich announces $7 billion investment in ten thousand new jobs in America.

FEBRUARY 9, 2017
DAY 21

* President Trump signs an executive order on a task force on crime reduction and public safety.
* President Trump signs an executive order on preventing violence against federal, state, tribal, and local law enforcement officers.
* President Trump signs an executive order on enforcing federal law with respect to transnational criminal organizations and preventing international trafficking.
* President Trump attends with Vice President Pence the swearing in of Jeff Sessions as attorney general.
* President Trump meets with top airline executives to discuss industry and jobs.
* Appeals court upholds the suspension of President Trump's temporary travel ban.
  Trump tweets, "See you in court; the security of our nation is at stake."

FEBRUARY 10, 2017
DAY 22

* Swearing-in ceremony for new secretary of health and human services director Tom Price.
* President Trump and Japanese prime minister Shinzo Abe hold their first official meeting today in Washington, DC, and affirm their strong determination to further strengthen the US-Japan alliance and economic relationship.
* President Trump approves the Oklahoma Disaster Declaration.
* President Trump speaks via phone with leaders of a few nations to discuss mutual issues.
* Appeals Court blocks Trump's bid to reinstate immigration order.
* President Trump and Shinzo Abe spend a weekend in Mar-a-Lago, Florida.

FEBRUARY 11, 2017
DAY 23

* President Trump plays golf with Prime Minister Abe of Japan and Ernie Els.
* President Trump holds a working dinner with Prime Minister Abe of Japan and his representatives at the winter White House in Mar-a-Lago, Florida.
President Trump states, "The US stands behind Japan 100 percent."

FEBRUARY 12, 2017
DAY 24

* President Trump is assessing all his legal options on the travel ban.
* President Trump returns to Washington, DC, after wrapping up the working weekend in Florida.
* President Trump defends immigration-enforcement raids.

FEBRUARY 13, 2017
DAY 25

* President Trump hosts Canadian prime minister Justin Trudeau to the White House and holds a joint press conference.
* President Trump and Prime Minister Justin Trudeau join women entrepreneurs at a round-table discussion. Ivanka Trump is in attendance.
* President Trump is evaluating the situation as Micheal Flynn, national security adviser, is under scrutiny amid reports that he spoke to the Russian ambassador about US sanctions.
* President Trump swears in Steven Mnuchin as the secretary of treasury.
* President Trump's national security adviser Michael Flynn resigns.

FEBRUARY 14, 2017
DAY 26

* President Trump meets with Secretary of Education Betsy DeVos, educators, parents, and teachers and holds a conference listening session.
  President Trump signs Executive Order House Joint Res. 41, eliminating a costly regulation that threatened to put domestic extraction companies and their employees at an unfair disadvantage.
* Happy Valentine's Day!
* Vice President Pence swears in new Veterans Affairs secretary director David Shulkin.
* Vice President Pence swears in new small business administrator Linda McMahon.

FEBRUARY 15, 2017
DAY 27

*   President Trump hosts Israeli prime minister Benjamin Netanyahu at the White House, and they jointly address a full press conference. Trump says, "Welcoming my friend Prime Minister Benjamin Netanyahu to the White House. With this visit the United States again reaffirms our unbreakable bond with our cherished ally, Israel. America and Israel are two nations that cherish the value of all human life."
    Netanyahu says, "Israel has no better ally than the United States, and I want to assure you the United States has no better ally than Israel. Let us seize this moment together."

*   President Trump meets with retail CEOs in the White House to discuss tax code reform.

FEBRUARY 16, 2017
DAY 28

* President Trump announces his new labor secretary nominee, Alexander Acosta.
* Mick Mulvaney is sworn in for the Office of Management and Budget, as budget chief.
* President Trump meets with House GOP supporters.
* President Trump signs H.J. Res. 38.
  "It will eliminate another terrible job-killing rule, saving many thousands of American jobs."
* President Trump holds a press conference.
  "The press has become so dishonest."
  "I inherited a mess."
  "Spoke with many foreign leaders."
  "Massive rebuilding of the Unites States military."
  "Keeping my promises to the American people."
  "We stood up for the men and women of law enforcement."
  "Border security measures—build a promised wall on the southern border."
  "Crack down on sanctuary cities."
  "I keep my campaign promises."
  "Taken steps to begin construction of the Keystone pipeline and Dakota access pipeline."
  "To drain the swamp of Washington, DC."
  "Repeal and replace Obamacare."
  "Ending the bleeding of jobs from our country."
* Question-and-answer session continues.

FEBRUARY 17, 2017
DAY 29

* The Senate confirms Scott Pruitt for the Environmental Protection Agency (EPA) chief.
* President Trump visits Boeing for a tour and speech. He is introduced to the new 787-10 Dreamliner airplane in North Charleston, South Carolina.

  "We're here today to celebrate American Engineering and American manufacturing."

  "We're also here today to celebrate jobs."

  "Rely less on imports and more on products made here in the USA."

  "Put our great people back to work."

  "Buy American; hire American."

  "We dream of things, and then we build them; we turn vision into reality."

  "Peace through strength."

  "I will not disappoint you."

  "Made in the USA. From now on it's going to be America first."

FEBRUARY 18, 2017
DAY 30

* President Trump will spend the weekend at Mar-a-Lago.
* President Trump holds a rally at the Melbourne International Airport. "I'm here today to tell you about our incredible progress in making America great again. I'm also here to tell you about our plans for the future and they are bold, and it's what our country is all about."

  "Two simple rules: buy American; hire American."

  "We don't give up; we never give up."

  "We have to keep our country safe."

  "We are going to drain the swamp in Washington, DC."

  "We are going to start winning again."

  "Now is the time."

  "We will make America great again."

FEBRUARY 19, 2017
DAY 31

* President Trump conducts a working weekend in Mar-a-Lago, Florida.
* President Trump interviews at least four candidates for national security adviser.

FEBRUARY 20, 2017
DAY 32

* President Trump announces US Army Lieutenant General Herbert Raymond McMaster as the new national security adviser.
* President Trump returns to Washington, DC.
* President's Day.

FEBRUARY 21, 2017
DAY 33

* President Trump visits the National African American History Museum and Culture in Washington, DC.

  "This museum is a beautiful tribute to so many American Heroes. This tour was a meaningful reminder of why we have to fight bigotry, intolerance, and hatred in all of its very ugly forms. The anti-Semitic threats targeting our Jewish community and community centers are horrible and are painful and a very sad reminder of the work that still must be done to root out hate and prejudice and evil."

* President Trump signs new immigration order.

  The president empowers the Department of Homeland Security to carry out the immigration laws currently on the books.

FEBRUARY 22, 2017
DAY 34

* President Trump holds a federal budget meeting at the White House. Mick Mulvaney is confirmed Budget Director.

   "The budget we are inheriting is a mess; the finances of our country are a mess, but we're going to clean it up."

   "We have enormous work to do as the national debt doubled over the last eight years."

   "We won't let your money be wasted anymore."

   "It's absolutely out of control, and we are going to do things that are going to be tremendous over the years."

* The Trump administration changes the transgender-student bathroom rules from the guidelines issued by the Obama administration.

FEBRUARY 23, 2017
DAY 35

* President Trump is involved in a listening session with leading manufacturing CEOs (twenty-four CEOs attend).
  "Bringing manufacturing back to America, creating high-wage jobs."
* President Trump is involved in a listening session on domestic and international human trafficking.
  "Focus on ending the absolutely horrific practice of human trafficking."

FEBRUARY 24, 2017
DAY 36

* President Trump blasts FBI leakers.
* President Trump meets with Peruvian president Pablo Kuczynski to discuss buying military equipment.
* President Trump signs an executive order to cut federal regulations.
  "Directs each agency to establish a Regulatory Reform Task Force, which will ensure that every agency is a team of dedicated and a real team of dedicated people to research all regulations that are unnecessary, burdensome, and harmful to the economy and therefore harmful to the creation of jobs and business."
* President Trump visits Conservative Political Action Conference (CPAC) and makes a speech.
  "They underestimated the power of the people."
  "We are fighting fake news."
  "Our victory was a win like nobody has seen before."
  "The victory and the win was dedicated to a country and people that believe in freedom, security, and the rule of law and conservative values."
  "We are a nation that will put our citizens first."
  "Basically, all I have done is kept my promises."
  "Secure border."
  "Support law enforcement."
  "Withdraw from TPP."
  "Repeal and replace Obamacare."
  "Construction of the Keystone and Dakota pipeline."
  "Lift the restrictions on American energy."
  "Reduce regulations."
  "Tax reform."
  "Bring jobs back to America."
  "Upgrade the military."
  "Obliterate ISIS."

"Keep Radical Islamic Terrorists out of our country."

"Meeting with many people and turning those meetings into action."

"Fix trade deals."

"Cut wasteful spending."

"Fix inner cities."

"Protect our Second Amendment"

"GOP will be the party of the American Worker."

FEBRUARY 25, 2017
DAY 37

* President Trump makes an announcement that he will not attend the Annual White House Correspondents Association Dinner in April.
* President Trump conducts a working lunch with Florida governor Rick Scott and Wisconsin governor Scott Walker to discuss the problems with Obamacare.
* President Trump visits Trump Hotel for dinner and surprises the press.

FEBRUARY 26, 2017
DAY 38

* President Trump and First Lady Melania Trump host the Annual
  Governors Ball. The theme is "Spring's Renewal." Forty-six governors
  attend.

FEBRUARY 27, 2017
DAY 39

*   President Trump attends the National Governors Association meeting and makes a speech.

"Increase in defense spending."

"We have to start winning wars again."

"Increase will be offset and paid for by finding greater savings and efficiencies across the federal government."

"We are going to do more with less."

"Keeping America safe, keeping out terrorists."

"Keeping out criminals and putting violent offenders behind bars or removing them from our country."

"Altogether we are getting the bad ones out."

"To restore the authority of the states."

"All states will benefit with our economic agenda."

"We have to fix our infrastructure."

"Repeal and replace Obamacare; Obamacare has failed."

"The tax cut is going to be major; it is going to be simple."

"Restore local control to our nation's education system."

"We are going to do these projects and so much more."

*   President Trump meets with health-insurance executives and conducts a listening session.

"Allowing this disaster [Obamacare] to continue is a mistake."

FEBRUARY 28, 2017
DAY 40

* President Trump signs an executive order about historically black colleges and universities (HBCUs) "to recognize the importance of Historically Black Colleges and Universities and to our shared mission of bringing education and opportunity to all of our people."
* President Trump signs executive order WOTUS (Waters of the United States), "directing the EPA to take action, paving the way for the elimination of this very destructive and horrible rule."
* President Trump signs H.R. 255: "The Promoting Women in Entrepreneurship Act enables the National Science Foundation to support women inventors."
* President Trump signs H.R. 321, the Inspire Women Act: "It ensures that the existing NASA programs recruit women to STEM-related jobs and aerospace careers."
* President Trump addresses Congress. The consensus is that President Trump just delivered the best speech of his political career and acted presidential.
* Vice President Pence swears in new commerce secretary, Wilbur Ross.

MARCH 1, 2017
DAY 41

* Ryan Zinke is confirmed as the secretary of the interior. He is sworn in by Vice President Pence.
* President Trump and congressional leaders will work together today to continue to chart a path forward on those issues from last night and more.
* President Trump has dinner with Secretary Tillerson.

MARCH 2, 2017
DAY 42

* President Trump tours USS *Gerald R. Ford* in Newport News, Virginia.

  The Newport News shipbuilders and USS *Gerald R. Ford* crew were on site for Trump's speech.

  "This is American craftsmanship at its biggest, at its best, at its finest. We will give the men and women of America's Armed Services the resources you need to keep us safe. We will have the finest equipment in the world. We are going to start winning again. To project American power in distant lands, hopefully its power we don't have to use, but if we do, they're in big big trouble. American ships will sail the seas, American planes will soar the skies, and American workers will build our fleets."

* Former Texas governor Rick Perry confirmed by Senate as the new energy secretary.

* Senate confirms Ben Carson to become secretary of the Department of Housing and Urban Development.

* Vice President Pence swears in Rick Perry and Ben Carson.

MARCH 3, 2017
DAY 43

*   President Trump conducts a listening-session conference with parents
and teachers at Saint Andrews Catholic School in Orlando, Florida.
"I asked Congress to support a school choice bill."

MARCH 4, 2017
DAY 44

* President Trump accuses former president Obama of wiretapping.
* Trump supporters organize and support Trump in cities around the United States in the "March 4 Trump."

MARCH 5, 2017
DAY 45

* President Trump calls for a Congressional investigation on claims that former president Obama had Trump Tower wiretapped during the election.

MARCH 6, 2017
DAY 46

* President Trump signs a revised version of an executive order regarding his travel ban. Includes the countries of Iran, Libya, Syria, Somalia, Sudan, and Yemen, and Iraq is not included in the revised version.
* President Trump announces that Exxon Mobil will be investing $20 billion in the Gulf Coast and the Gulf Coast region. It will create forty-five thousand great jobs—paying $100,000 on average.
* President Trump proclaims March 5 to March 11, 2017, as National Consumer Protection Week.

MARCH 7, 2017
DAY 47

* President Trump and Representative Steve Scalise meet with the US House Deputy Whip team on Obamacare replacement.
  "Obamacare is collapsing and it's in bad shape, and we're going to take action."
* A plan to repeal and replace Obamacare has begun. The House GOP Health Care Bill is proposed.

MARCH 8, 2017
DAY 48

* President Trump plans a dinner with Senator Ted Cruz.
* President Trump and First Lady Melania Trump announce that the 139th White House Easter Egg Roll will take place on Monday, April 17, 2017.
* President Trump meets with Congressman Elijah Cummings (D) to discuss rising drug prices.
* President Trump meets with Laurene Powell Jobs, the founder and president of Emerson Collective. They discuss education and immigration policy.
* President Trump holds a strategic-affairs lunch with leaders in the private sector to discuss infrastructure.
* International Women's Day and Women's History Month.
* CIA documents are released by WikiLeaks.
* Lindsey Graham and Sheldon Whitehouse send a letter to the FBI director and the attorney general for information on President Trump's wiretapping accusations against Obama.
* Hawaii launches the first lawsuit over the revised travel ban.

MARCH 9, 2017
DAY 49

* President Trump meets with his National Economic Council and CEOs of community banks for a listening session.
  "We like to preserve our Community Banks."
* Legal challenges begin from several states regarding President Trump's revised travel ban.
  Washington, Massachusetts, New York, Oregon, and Minnesota join a lawsuit with Hawaii on the revised travel ban.
* Paul Ryan presents a PowerPoint presentation on the American Health Care Act to replace Obamacare.

MARCH 10, 2017
DAY 50

* President Trump meets with House Committee chairmen regarding the GOP Health Care Bill, the American Health Care Act.
* The White House has a three-pronged approach to America's health care crisis:
  1. Repeal and replace Obamacare.
  2. Provide essential regulatory relief.
  3. Reform health care through additional legislation.
* Jobs report shows there have been two hundred thirty-five thousand new jobs added to the economy, and the unemployment rate ticks down to 4.7 percent.

MARCH 11, 2017
DAY 51

* President Trump has lunch with White House staff and cabinet members at Trump's National Golf Club in Sterling, Virginia.
* President Trump orders forty-six US attorneys to resign. US Attorney Preet Bharara is fired because he does not resign.

MARCH 12, 2017
DAY 52

* Vice President Pence is in Louisville, Kentucky, regarding Obamacare.
* Trump officials discuss the effort to repeal and replace Obamacare on all the Sunday talk shows.

MARCH 13, 2017
DAY 53

* President Trump signs H.R. 609, which designates the Department of Veterans Affairs Health Care Center in Center Township, Butler County, Pennsylvania, as the Abie Abraham VA Clinic.
* President Trump signs an executive order to reorganize the Executive Branch.
  "Drain the swamp."
  "A long overdue reorganization of our Federal Departments and Agencies."
  "We want to empower them [selected cabinets] to make their agencies as lean and effective as possible."
* President Trump holds a listening session on health care.
  "The fact is, Obamacare is a disaster."
* President Trump holds his first cabinet meeting.
* Introduced H.J. Res. 66—disapproving the rule submitted by the Department of Labor relating to savings arrangements established by states for nongovernmental employees.
* Introduced H.J. Res. 67—disapproving the rule submitted by the Department of Labor relating to savings arrangements established by qualified state political subdivisions for nongovernmental employees.

MARCH 14, 2017
DAY 54

* President Trump hosts the deputy crown prince and minister of defense of the kingdom of Saudi Arabia at the White House.
* President Trump's 2005 tax return gets revealed on an MSNBC show from a reporter's mailbox.
* Vice President Pence swears in Seema Verma, who will become the fifteenth administrator of the Centers for Medicare and Medicaid Services.

MARCH 15, 2017
DAY 55

* President Trump visits the American Center for Mobility in Detroit, Michigan.

  The president is delivering on his promise to bring back jobs and rebuild America's manufacturing base, and this is only the beginning. "Buy American, and Hire American."

* President Trump announced that the EPA and the National Highway Traffic Safety Administration (NHTSA) are reinstating the midterm evaluation of the corporate average fuel economy and greenhouse gas emissions standards for the automotive industry.

* President Trump holds a rally in Nashville, Tennessee.

* President Trump is interviewed by Fox host Tucker Carlson.

* A federal judge in Hawaii puts President Trump's revised travel ban on hold—Judge Derrick Watson of the US District Court, District of Hawaii.

MARCH 16, 2017
DAY 56

* President Trump meets with Irish leader Taoiseach Enda Kenny to discuss the ties between both countries.
* President Trump attends the Friends of Ireland luncheon.
* President Trump approves the California Disaster Declaration.
* President Trump's fiscal budget is presented to Congress with a military spending increase and domestic programs spending cuts.
* President Trump wishes a happy birthday to the oldest living Pearl Harbor Veteran, Ray Chavez.
* Senator Dan Coats gets sworn in by Vice President Pence; he will become the fifth director of National Intelligence.
* The House Budget Committee approves the American Health Care Act to move it forward.

MARCH 17, 2017
DAY 57

*   President Trump meets with German chancellor Angela Merkel to discuss mutual issues.
*   President Trump attends a listening session with Veterans Affairs and VA secretary Shulkin and representatives from the various veterans-service organizations.
*   President Trump, Congressman Steve Scalise, and Congressman Mark Walker attend a Republican Study Committee meeting regarding health care and the improvements that are being made.
*   President Trump leads a round-table discussion on vocational training with American and German business leaders.
*   Happy Saint Patrick's Day!

MARCH 18, 2017
DAY 58

* President Trump spends the weekend at Mar-a-Lago.
* President Trump addresses issues regarding the Department of Veterans Affairs.
* The Secret Service apprehends a person who jumps a bike rack around the White House buffer zone.

MARCH 19, 2017
DAY 59

* President Trump holds meetings regarding North Korea and China and meets with military personnel.
* Sunday talk shows state that there is no evidence to back President Trump's claim that former president Barack Obama wiretapped him.

MARCH 20, 2017
DAY 60

* President Trump meets with Bill Gates.
* President Trump welcomes Prime Minister Haider al-Abadi of Iraq.
* FBI director James Comey appears before the House Intelligence Committee regarding wiretapping and the Russian involvement during the presidential election.
* Confirmation hearings in the Judiciary Committee begin for the president's Supreme Court nominee, Judge Neil Gorsuch.
* President Trump holds a Make America Great Again rally in Louisville, Kentucky.
* Donald Trump delegated the Presidential Memorandum for the Secretary of State on the Declaration of Authority under the National Defense Authorization Act for the fiscal year 2017.

MARCH 21, 2017
DAY 61

* President Trump signs S.442, the National Aeronautics and Space Administration Transition Authorization Act of 2017.
* President Trump meets with the Republican House Conference.
* President Trump hosts a Legislative Affairs group meeting.
* President Trump attends the National Republican Congressional Committee March dinner.
* President Trump proclaims March 21, 2017, as National Agriculture Day.

MARCH 22, 2017
DAY 62

* President Trump attends the Women in Healthcare Panel hosted by Seema Verma.
* President Trump meets with the Congressional Black Caucus Executive Committee.
* President Trump sends best wishes to all those around the world celebrating the wonderful ancient holiday of Nowruz, "New Day."
* President Trump approves the Wyoming Disaster Declaration.
* President Trump calls Prime Minister Theresa May of the United Kingdom, expressing his condolences on the terror attack in London.
* The White House makes financial disclosures public.
* President Trump has dinner with Secretary of State Tillerson.
* House intel chairman says, "President's personal communications may have been collected."

MARCH 23, 2017
DAY 63

* The House postpones the vote on the health-care bill.
* President Trump would like a vote on Friday regarding the American Health Care Act.
* President Trump meets with the House Freedom Caucus members.
* President Trump holds a listening session with American truckers and CEOs regarding health care.
* President Trump determines that it is necessary to continue the national emergency declared in Executive Order 13664 with respect to South Sudan.

MARCH 24, 2017
DAY 64

* Obamacare Repeal Bill fails for a vote. Speaker Paul Ryan pulls the legislation from a vote.

   "We had no Democrat support. Obamacare, unfortunately, will explode."

* President Trump signs a presidential permit so construction can begin on the Keystone XL Pipeline.

   Trans Canada will finally be allowed to complete this project.

   Keystone XL Pipeline will span nine hundred miles and can deliver eight hundred thousand barrels per day to the Gulf Coast refineries.

* President Trump hosts a Greek Independence Day celebration.

* President Trump meets with twenty-five Medal of Honor recipients at the White House.

* The US District Court for the Eastern District of Virginia upholds the president's revised executive order protecting the nation from foreign people who seek to do us harm in the United States. The order, U.S. District Judge Anthony Trenga wrote in his opinion, falls well within the president's authority over the country's foreign policy and national security.

* The chairman and CEO of Charter Communications, Tom Rutledge, makes a job announcement: invest $25 billion, create twenty thousand jobs, and relocate offshore call centers to the United States, which will create six hundred new jobs.

* President Trump proclaims March 25, 2017, as Greek Independence Day, a national day of celebration of Greek and American democracy.

MARCH 25, 2017
DAY 65

* President Trump tweets, "Obamacare will explode and we will all get together and piece together a great health care plan for the people. Do not worry."
* President Trump stays in the Washington, DC, area and visits Trump National Golf Club in Sterling, Virginia, for a working weekend.
* Medal of Honor Day.
* It is the 196th anniversary of Greek independence.

MARCH 26, 2017
DAY 66

* The House Freedom Caucus does not support voting on the Obamacare Repeal Bill.
* President Trump does not blame Speaker Paul Ryan.

MARCH 27, 2017
DAY 67

* President Trump participates in a round table with women small-business owners.
* President Trump selects Jared Kushner (son-in-law) to head a White House office to examine the way the federal government operates called the White House Office of American Innovation (OAI).
* President Trump signs into law H.J. RES 37, H.J. RES 44, H.J. RES 57, and H.J. RES 58.

  House Joint Resolution 37 rolls back the so-called blacklisting rule.

  House Joint Resolution 44 removes a Bureau of Land Management rule that took control of land-use decisions away from states and local decision makers and gave it to Washington, and that's not good.

  House Joint Resolutions 57 and 58 eliminate harmful burdens on state and local taxes on school systems that could have cost states hundreds of millions of dollars. So we're removing these additional layers of bureaucracy to encourage more freedom and innovation in our schools.
* President Trump signs executive order on the revocation of federal contracting executive orders.
* Jeff Sessions on defunding sanctuary cities: "If they don't follow the rule of law, they will be defunded."

MARCH 28, 2017
DAY 68

* President Trump signs an executive order on environmental-regulations elimination to create energy independence and economic growth.
* President Trump approves the Nevada Disaster Declaration.
* President Trump attends a reception for senators and their spouses.
* President Trump hosts a listening session with the Fraternal Order of Police.
* President Trump calls German chancellor Angela Merkel to congratulate her on the Saarland State election on March 26, 2017.
* President Trump calls Prime Minister Narendra Modi, of India, to congratulate him on winning India's recent state-level elections.
* President Trump signs S. 305 into law.
  S. 305, the Vietnam War Veterans Recognition Act of 2017, encourages the display of the US flag on March 29, National Vietnam War Veterans Day.
* Ford Motor Company in Michigan announced it will create 130 jobs and invest $1.2 billion at plants in Flat Rock, Romeo, and Wayne Wochit.

MARCH 29, 2017
DAY 69

* President Trump holds a listening session on opioid abuse. New Jersey governor Chris Christie is the leader to combat the opioid crisis.
* President Trump visits the Women's Empowerment Panel.
* A federal judge in Hawaii puts an indefinite hold on President Trump's executive order that was issued on national security.
* The Department of Justice reviews the ruling and considers the best way to defend the president's lawful and necessary executive order.

MARCH 30, 2017
DAY 70

* President Trump meets with the prime minister of Denmark, Lars Lokke Rasmussen.
* President Trump hosts a legislative-affairs lunch on opioid and drug abuse.
* President Trump tweets, "The Freedom Caucus will hurt the entire Republican agenda if they don't get on the team and fast. We must fight them and Dems in 2018!"
* President Trump holds a meeting with Treasury Secretary Steve Mnuchin, the National Economic Council, and the president's team to address the tax-reform debate.

MARCH 31, 2017
DAY 71

* President Trump meets with former secretary of state Condoleezza Rice.

* President Trump announces his intent to nominate Carlos G. Muniz to the Department of Education.

* President Trump attends a listening session with the National Association of Manufacturers.

  "My Administration is working every day to make it easier for manufacturers to build, hire, and grow in America. The National Association of Manufacturers survey shows that 93 percent of manufacturers now have a positive outlook on the future of their business in this country."

* President Trump meets with the director of the National Institutes of Health.

* President Trump meets with the director of the Office of Management and Budget.

* President Trump signs an executive order on establishing enhanced collection and enforcement of antidumping and countervailing duties and violations of trade and customs laws.

  "I'm signing an executive order to ensure that we fully collect all duties imposed on foreign importers that cheat."

* President Trump signs an executive order regarding the Omnibus Report on significant trade deficits.

  "Free and fair trade is critical to the nation's prosperity, national security, and foreign policy. I'm ordering the first-ever comprehensive review of America's trade deficits and all violations of trade rules that harm the United States and the workers of the United States."

* President Trump signs an executive order on providing an order of succession within the Department of Justice.

* President Trump signs into law H.J. Res. 42, which nullifies the Department of Labor's Federal-State Unemployment Comprehensive

Program; Middle Class Tax Relief and Job Creation Act of 2012 provision on establishing appropriate occupations for drug testing of unemployment-compensation applicants.

* President Trump signs into law H.R. 1362, which designates the Department of Veterans Affairs community-based outpatient clinic in Pago Pago, American Samoa, the Fa Leomavaegu Eni Fa' aua' a Hunkin VA clinic.

* President Trump signs into law S.J. Res. 1, which approves the location of a memorial to commemorate and honor the members of the Armed Forces who served on active duty in support of Operation Desert Storm and Operation Desert Shield.

* President Trump proclaims April 2017 as National Sexual Assault Awareness and Prevention Month.

* President Trump proclaims April 2017 as National Financial Capability Month.

* President Trump proclaims April 2017 as Cancer Control Month.

* President Trump proclaims April 2017 as National Child Abuse Prevention Month.

* President Trump proclaims April 2017 as National Donate Life Month.

* President Trump proclaims April 2, 2017, as World Autism Awareness Day.

* The Department of Justice files an appeal in the Ninth Circuit to Hawaii's federal judge's preliminary injunction against the president's lawful and necessary executive order dealing with the protection of the country.

APRIL 1, 2017
DAY 72

*   President Trump tweets out regarding fake news coverage.

APRIL 2, 2017
DAY 73

* President Trump hits the links with Republican senator Rand Paul to discuss repealing and replacing Obamacare.
* President Trump approves the California Disaster Declaration.
* The White House is lit in blue in honor of World Autism Awareness Day in Washington, DC.

APRIL 3, 2017
DAY 74

* Egyptian president Abdel Fattah al-Sisi visits President Trump at the White House. They discuss the fight on terrorism.
* President Trump donates $78,333.32, his salary, to the Park Service. The check is presented to the secretary of the interior, Ryan Zinke, and the superintendent of the Harper's Ferry park site, Brandy Burg.
* President Trump meets with Secretary of State Rex Tillerson.
* President Trump proclaims April 2 through April 8, 2017, as National Crime Victim's Rights Week.
* President Trump issues a memorandum for the National Commission on Military, National, and Public Service outlining principles for reforming the military selective service process.
* President Trump announces his intent to nominate Dan R. Brouillette to the Department of Energy.
* President Trump calls President Pedro Pablo Kuczynski, of Peru, to express condolences for the tragic loss of life and devastation in Peru due to the flooding and landslides.
* President Trump calls President Juan Manuel Santos, of Columbia, to express condolences for the devastation caused by the country's recent mudslides.
* President Trump calls President Vladimir Putin, of Russia, to condemn the attack in Saint Petersburg.
* President Trump signs into law H.J. Res. 69, which nullifies the Department of the Interior's Fish and Wildlife Service's final rule relating to nonsubsistence takings of wildlife on National Wildlife Refuges in Alaska.
* President Trump signs into law H.J. Res. 83, which nullifies the Department of Labor's rule titled Clarification of Employer's Continuing Obligation to make and maintain an accurate record of each recordable injury and illness.

* President Trump signs into law H.R. 1228, which provides for the appointment of members of the Board of Directors of the Office of Compliance to replace members whose terms expire during March and May 2017.
* President Trump signs into law S.J. Res. 34, which nullifies the Federal Communications Commission's Rule on privacy of customers of broadband and other telecommunications services.

APRIL 4, 2017
DAY 75

* President Trump promotes his "America First" plan at the 2017 North America's Building Trades Unions National Legislative Conference.
* President Trump blames Assad for the chemical attack in Syria.
* President Trump hosts a CEO town hall on the American business climate.
* President Trump meets with the administrator of the Environmental Protection Agency Scott Pruitt, with Secretary of the Treasury Steve Mnuchin and with Secretary of Housing and Urban Development Ben Carson.
* President Trump announces intent to nominate Heath P. Tarbert to the Department of the Treasury.
* President Trump's nominations are delivered to the Senator Sigal Mandelken of New York to be the undersecretary for terrorism and financial crimes, since David S. Cohen resigned. Heath P. Tarbert of Maryland is to become the assistant secretary of the Treasury vice Marisa Lago.

APRIL 5, 2017
DAY 76

* President Trump removes Steve Bannon from the National Security Council.
* President Trump holds a news conference with King Abdullah II of Jordan. First Lady Melania Trump hosts Queen Rania of Jordan.
* President Trump denounces the chemical attack in Syria.
* President Trump believes the former national security adviser Susan Rice committed a crime.
* President Trump makes a proclamation honoring the memory of John Glenn.
* President Trump calls Chancellor Angela Merkel, of Germany, to discuss several issues of mutual concern and interest.
* President Trump calls Prime Minister Shinzo Abe, of Japan, to discuss regional matters of concern.
* President Trump implements executive order 13771, titled "Reducing Regulation and Controlling Regulatory Costs."

APRIL 6, 2017
DAY 77

* President Trump orders a missile attack against Syria.
* President Trump meets with wounded warriors at the White House.
* President Trump heads out to Mar-a-Lago to host Chinese president Xi Jinping and Madame Peng Liyuan.
* Republicans invoke "nuclear option" for Supreme Court Gorsuch confirmation.
* President Trump sends a message to Congress regarding the continuation of the national emergency with respect to Somalia.
* President Trump announces his intent to nominate Derek Kan to the Department of Transportation.
* Nominations sent to the Senate:
  Makan Delrahim of California to be the assistant attorney general, vice William Joseph Baer, who resigned.
  Eric D. Hargan of Illinois to be deputy secretary of Health and Human Services, vice William V. Corr, who resigned.
  David L. Norquist of Virginia to be undersecretary of defense (comptroller), vice Michael J. McCord.

APRIL 7, 2017
DAY 78

* President Trump concludes his meeting with Chinese president Xi Jinping at Mar-a-Lago.
* Supreme Court nominee, Neil Gorsuch, is confirmed by the Senate. President Trump congratulates him.
* President Trump draws wide political support on the decision to strike Syria in retaliation for the use of chemical weapons on its own people.
* President Trump proclaims April 7, 2017, as Education and Sharing Day.
* The White House announces 2017 spring garden tours.
* President Trump announces intent to nominate personnel to key administration posts:
  Vishal J. Amin of Michigan to be intellectual property enforcement coordinator in the Executive Office of the President.
  Mark E. Green of Tennessee to be secretary of the army.
  Kevin Allen Hassett of Massachusetts to be a member and chair of the Council of Economic Advisors.
  Stephen T. Parente of Minnesota to be an assistant secretary of Health and Human Services, Planning, and Evaluation.
  Neomi Rao of Washington, DC, to be the administrator of the Office of Information and Regulatory Affairs, Office of Management and Budget.
  Russell Vought of Virginia to be deputy director of the Office of Management and Budget.
* President Trump proclaims April 14, 2017, as Pan American Day and April 9 through April 15, 2017, as Pan American Week.
* President Trump proclaims April 9, 2017, as National Former Prisoner of War Recognition Day.

APRIL 8, 2017
DAY 79

* President Trump provides Congress his justification for the Syria missile strike under the War Powers Resolution.
* Jared Kushner and Steve Bannon hold a meeting to end the White House rift.
* President Trump calls King Salman bin Abd al-Aziz Al Saud, of the Kingdom of Saudi Arabia, to discuss the military strike and joint relationship.
* President Trump sends a letter regarding missile strike to the Speaker of the House of Representatives and the president pro tempore of the Senate.
* President Trump calls Acting President Hwang Kyo-Ahn, of South Korea, to discuss military strike and joint relationship.
  President Trump announces his intent to nominate Lee Francis Cissna of Maryland as director of the US Citizenship and Immigration Services.

APRIL 9, 2017
DAY 80

* President Trump calls Prime Minster Shinzo Abe, of Japan, on the recent developments in Syria.

* President Trump calls President al Sisi, of Egypt, to convey his deepest condolences to Egypt and to the families who lost loved ones in the terrorist attacks against Christian churches on Palm Sunday.

* President Trump calls the commanding officers of the USS *Ross*, Commander Russell Caldwell, and the USS *Porter*, Commander Andria Slough, to thank them and their personnel for successfully executing the strike against the Shayrat Air Base in Syria.

* President Trump calls Prime Minister Stefan Lofven, of Sweden, to express condolences to the loved ones of those who were killed in Friday's terrorist attack in central Stockholm.

APRIL 10, 2017
DAY 81

* Neil Gorsuch is sworn in as the next Supreme Court justice.
* President Trump meets with the director of the Office of Management and Budget, Mick Mulvaney.

APRIL 11, 2017
DAY 82

* The White House states, "There is evidence that Syria used a sarin nerve agent, and Russia is linked to Assad to cover up the illegal use of chemical weapons."
* President Trump leads a strategic and policy CEO discussion. "At the top of our agenda is the creation of great high-paying jobs for American workers."
* President Trump meets with the secretary of homeland security John Kelly, national security adviser H.R. McMaster, and national economic council director Gary Cohn.
* President Trump has a working dinner with senior military leaders.
* President Trump sends a letter to the president of the Senate regarding Montenegro's NATO Accession Protocol.
* President Trump declares his intent to nominate personnel to key administration posts:
  Marshall Billingslea of Virginia to be assistant secretary for Terrorist Financing, Department of the Treasury.
  Gilbert B. Kaplan of Washington, DC, to be undersecretary of commerce for International Trade.
  John Marshall Mitnick of Virginia to be general counsel at the Department of Homeland Security.
  John J. Sullivan of Maryland to be deputy secretary of state and to serve concurrently and without additional compensation as deputy secretary of state for Management and Resources.

APRIL 12, 2017
DAY 83

* President Trump meets with NATO secretary general Jens Soltenberg. President Trump reaffirms the strong commitment of the United States to NATO.
* President Trump states, "Billions and billions are being wasted on activities that are not delivering results for hardworking American taxpayers."
* President Trump issues a memorandum for the director of FBI regarding delegation of authority under the National Defense Authorization Act for Fiscal Year 2017.

APRIL 13, 2017
DAY 84

* The US military at approximately 7:00 p.m. launches a military air strike using the MOAB (the Mother of All Bombs) on an ISIS tunnel complex in Afghanistan. It is the largest nonnuclear weapon ever used in combat by the US military. The bomb weighed twenty-one thousand pounds, and the explosive yield is equivalent to eleven tons of TNT.
* President Trump meets with the I-85 bridge first responders.
* President Trump signs H.J. Res. 43 into law, which nullifies the Department of Health and Human Services rule prohibiting recipients of the Title X grants for the provision of Family Planning Services from excluding a subgrantee from participating for reasons other than its ability to provide Title X services.
* President Trump signs H.J. Res. 63 into law, which nullifies the Department of Labor's rule on savings arrangements established by Qualified State Political Subdivisions for nongovernmental employees.

APRIL 14, 2017
DAY 85

* President Trump heads to Mar-a-Lago.
* President Trump proclaims April 15 through April 23, 2017, as National Park Week.
* President Trump announces his intent to nominate personnel to key administration posts:

  Scott Garrett of New Jersey to be president of the Export-Import Bank for a term of four years, expiring January 20, 2021.

  Spencer Bachus III of Alabama to be a member of the board of directors of the Export-Import Bank for a term of four years.
* Vice President Pence traveled to South Korea, Japan, Indonesia, and Australia. Key themes will be security alliances and economic engagements. Second Lady Karen Pence will also travel and highlight her initiative, art therapy; meet with military service members and spouses; and participate in cultural activities.

APRIL 15, 2017
DAY 86

* North Korea missile launch fails.
* Protestors gather at rallies demanding President Trump release his tax returns.
* President Trump spends Easter weekend in Mar-a-Lago.

APRIL 16, 2017
DAY 87

* President Trump's administration hopes China can rein in North Korea.
* President Trump will not release his tax returns anytime soon.
* Vice President Pence and Mrs. Pence address the troops in Seoul, South Korea.

APRIL 17, 2017
DAY 88

* President Trump attends the White House Easter Egg Roll.

* President Trump makes a call to President Recep Tayyip Erdogan, of Turkey, to discuss US action regarding Syria and its counter-ISIS campaign.

* Vice President Pence visits soldiers at the Demilitarized Zone, Republic of Korea.

* Vice President Pence meets with Speaker of the National Assembly Chung Sye-Kyun.

* Vice President Pence holds joint news conference with Acting President Hwang, of South Korea.

APRIL 18, 2017
DAY 89

* President Trump arrives in Milwaukee, Wisconsin.
* President Trump visits the manufacturer Snap-On Tools in Kenosha, Wisconsin.
* President Trump signs Executive Order Buy American; Hire American.
* President Trump signs H.R. 353 into law, the Weather Research and Forecasting Innovation Act of 2017.
* President Trump receives a call from Prime Minister Theresa May, of the United Kingdom, regarding her plans to call a special election in June.
* Vice President Pence meets with Deputy Prime Minister Taro Aso to launch the US-Japan economic dialogue in Tokyo, Japan.

APRIL 19, 2017
DAY 90

* President Trump welcomes the Super Bowl LI champion New England Patriots to the White House.
* President Trump signs the Veterans Choice Program Extension and Improvement Act, S. 544.
* President Trump meets with secretary of Veterans Affairs David Shulkin.
* President Trump meets with national security adviser H. R. McMaster.
* President Trump signs into law the following resolutions:

  S.J. Res. 30, which reappoints Steve Case as a citizen regent of the board of regents of the Smithsonian Institution.

  S.J. Res. 35, which appoints Michael Govan as a citizen regent of the board of regents of the Smithsonian Institution.

  S.J. Res. 36, which appoints Roger W. Ferguson as a citizen regent of the board of regents of the Smithsonian Institution.

APRIL 20, 2017
DAY 91

* President Trump welcomes Italian prime minister Paolo Gentiloni to the White House.
* President Trump to nominate Scott Brown as ambassador to New Zealand.
* President Trump signs a memorandum regarding the investigation pursuant to Section 232(B) of the Trade Expansion Act and a presidential memorandum for the secretary of commerce regarding steel imports and threats to national security.
* Vice President Pence meets with Vice President Jusuf Kalla and Indonesian cabinet ministers in Jakarta, Indonesia.
* Vice President Pence holds a press conference with Indonesian president Joko Widodo.
* Vice President Pence visits ASEAN (the Association of Southeast Asian Nations).
* Vice President Pence participates in an interfaith dialogue in Jakarta, Indonesia.

APRIL 21, 2017
DAY 92

* President Trump meets with Secretary of State Rex Tillerson.
* President Trump meets with Secretary of the Treasury Steve Mnuchin.
* President Trump meets with the director of the Office of Management and Budget Mick Mulvaney.
* President Trump signs three financial services (presidential actions):
  1. Identifying and reducing tax regulatory burdens
  2. The subject of financial stability, the overnight council
  3. Orderly liquidation authority
* President Trump approves the Utah Disaster Declaration.
* President Trump approves the Washington Disaster Declaration.
* President Trump approves the Idaho Disaster Declaration.
* President Trump announces his intent to nominate the following key additions to his administration:

  Brett Giroir of Texas to be an assistant secretary of Health and Human Services.

  Heather L. MacDougall of Florida to be a member of the Occupational Safety and Health Review Commission.

  Elinore F. McCance-Katz of Rhode Island to be assistant secretary for Mental Health and Substance Use, Department of Health and Human Services.

  Neal J. Rackleff of Texas to be an assistant secretary of Housing and Urban Development, Community Planning and Development.

  Philip A. Miscimarra of Illinois to be chairman of the National Labor Relations Board.
* President Trump proclaims April 23 through April 29, 2017, as National Volunteer Week.

APRIL 22, 2017
DAY 93

* President Trump issues a statement on Earth Day:
  "This April 22nd, as we observe Earth Day, I hope that our nation can come together to give thanks for the land we all love and call home."
* President Trump visits Walter Reed National Military Medical Center. President Trump awards a Purple Heart to a soldier injured in Afghanistan and visits with wounded military personnel.

APRIL 23, 2017
DAY 94

* President Trump plans a busy week ahead as his one-hundredth day approaches.

* President Trump makes a call to Prime Minister Shinzo Abe, of Japan, addressing a range of regional and global issues.

APRIL 24, 2017
DAY 95

* President Trump makes a statement regarding Armenian Remembrance Day 2017.
* President Trump makes a call to President Xi Jinping, of China, regarding issues with North Korea.
* President Trump holds a video conference with NASA astronauts aboard the National Space Station and congratulates astronaut Peggy Whitson for breaking the record for cumulative time spent in space by a US astronaut.
* President Trump holds a working lunch with ambassadors of countries on the UN Security Council.
* President Trump signs a proclamation on Holocaust remembrance.
* President Trump holds a credential ceremony for newly appointed ambassadors to Washington, DC.
* President Trump meets with chairman of the Joint Chiefs of Staff Joseph Dunford.
* President Trump participates in a reception with conservative media.
* President Trump has dinner with Senator McCain, Mrs. McCain, and Senator Graham.
* President Trump holds a call with Chancellor Angela Merkel, of Germany, and discusses a wide range of issues.
* President Trump announces his intent to nominate key administration posts:
  Brett Giroir of Texas to be an assistant secretary of Health and Human Services.
  Heather L. MacDougall of Florida to be a member of the Occupational Safety and Health Review Commission.
  Elinore F. McCance-Katz of Rhode Island to be assistant secretary for Mental Health and Substance Use.
  Neal J. Rackleff of Texas to be assistant secretary of Housing and Urban Development.
  Philip A. Miscimarra of Illinois to be chairman of the National Labor Relations Board.

APRIL 25, 2017
DAY 96

* President Trump participates in the US Holocaust Memorial Museum's National Days of Remembrance.
* President Trump meets with Secretary of the Treasury Steven Mnuchin.
* President Trump holds a meeting on tax reform.
* President Trump holds a farmer's round table and signs an executive order promoting agriculture and rural prosperity in America.
* President Trump meets with National Security Adviser H. R. McMaster.
* Deputy Secretary of Commerce, Vice Bruce H. Andrews, resigns.
* President Trump announces appointment of Randolph D. Alles to be director of the US Secret Service.
* President Trump calls Prime Minister Justin Trudeau, of Canada, to discuss dairy trade in Wisconsin, New York State, and various other areas.

APRIL 26, 2017
DAY 97

* President Trump signs antiquities executive order.
* President Trump has lunch with Vice President Pence.
* President Trump meets with Secretary of State Rex Tillerson.
* President Trump signs the education federalism executive order.
* President Trump briefs senators regarding North Korea.
* President Trump holds a National Teacher of the Year event.
* President Trump proposes a massive tax cut for the American people.
* President Trump calls President Pena Nieto, of Mexico, and Prime Minister Trudeau, of Canada.

APRIL 27, 2017
DAY 98

* President Trump welcomes President Mauricio Macri and Mrs. Macri of Argentina and has a working lunch with them.
* President Trump signs a memorandum on aluminum imports and threats to national security.
* President Trump signs an executive order on improving accountability and whistle-blower protection.

APRIL 28, 2017
DAY 99

* President Trump makes remarks at the National Rifle Association Leadership Forum.
* President Trump signs an executive order on an America-first offshore energy strategy.
* President Trump proclaims May 1, 2017, as Loyalty Day.
* President Trump proclaims May 2017 as National Physical Fitness and Sports Month.
* President Trump proclaims April 30 through May 6, 2017, as Small Business Week.
* President Trump proclaims April 30 through May 6, 2017, as National Charter Schools Week.
* President Trump signs H.J. Res. 99 into law.
* President Trump proclaims May 2017 as Older Americans Month.
* President Trump proclaims May 2017 as Jewish American Heritage Month.
* President Trump proclaims May 2017 as National Foster Care Month.
* President Trump proclaims May 2017 as Asian American and Pacific Islander Heritage Month.

APRIL 29, 2017
DAY 100

* President Trump signs an executive order on the establishment of the Office of Trade and Manufacturing Policy.
* President Trump signs an executive order addressing trade agreement violations and abuses.
* President Trump calls President Rodrigo Duterte of the Philippines to discuss the concerns of ASEAN regarding regional security, including the threat posed by North Korea. They also discussed the fact that the Philippine government is fighting very hard to rid its country of drugs.

Chapter 8

THE UNITED STATES' FINANCIAL/ POPULATION STATUS ON APRIL 29, 2017

Donald J. Trump took office on January 20, 2017, and the key financial data of the United States of America is listed below for day 100 of his presidency. After one hundred days of the Trump presidency, compare the key financial data of the United States of America presented in chapter 4 and see if his presidency was positive or negative on the country.

US Population	324,958,191
US Workforce	153,132,102
Official Unemployed	7,141,741
Actual Unemployed	14,152,817
US Trade Deficit	$741,450,317,900
US National Debt	$19,893,007,500,000
Debt per Citizen	$61,222
Debt per Taxpayer	$165,654
Mortgage Rate	4.19 percent (Thirty-year fixed)
Unemployment Rate	4.5 percent
Inflation Rate	2.4 percent
US Savings Rate	5.60 percent
Dow	20940.51
S+P 500	2384.20
NASDAQ	6047.61

RESOURCES

United States Census
United States Treasury
Bureau of Labor Statistics
Federal Reserve
United States Presidential Election Results, 2016 Wikipedia
Whitehouse.gov
Internet searches
Internet videos
Local and national news broadcasts